HOWL
LIKE A
WOLF!

Kathleen Yale

Illustrated by Kaley McKean

Storey Publishing

FOR ATTICUS AND ROSARIO

May imagination, curiosity, and wonder
guide you always.

———————————————

The mission of Storey Publishing is to serve our customers by
publishing practical information that encourages
personal independence in harmony with the environment.

Edited by Hannah Fries and Michal Lumsden
Art direction and book design by Alethea Morrison
Cover and interior illustrations by © Kaley McKean

Storey Publishing
210 MASS MoCA Way
North Adams, MA 01247
storey.com

Printed in China by R.R. Donnelley
10 9 8 7 6 5 4 3 2 1

LIBRARY OF CONGRESS CATALOGING-IN-
PUBLICATION DATA ON FILE

CONTENTS

HOWL like a
WOLF

WHAT BIG TEETH YOU HAVE!
A wolf's teeth are sharp, big, and heavy. They look a lot like your pet dog's teeth, but wolves' jaws are much stronger. In fact, the force of their bite is strong enough to break bones.

Ayhooooooooo! Hear me howl! I'm a gray wolf. Well, that's my name, but actually, my thick, warm fur can be gray, brown, black, or even pure white.

I'm a social animal, so I like to hang out with my fellow wolves. I live in a pack with my parents, older siblings, and littermates. My parents are the alphas — that means they're in charge — and the rest of us follow their lead.

Most of the time our pack is on the move, hunting and patrolling the borders of our territory. In fact, we often run 10 to 20 miles a day — even up to 50 miles when we need to. On our way, we pee and poop at the edges of our range so that when other wolf packs smell our markings, they know to keep out. It's kind of like having a fence around your backyard.

We hunt together for large prey like deer, elk, moose, and bison, but we chase smaller prey like rabbits, squirrels, and mice, too. We hunt in order to eat, but we don't kill for fun, and we rarely waste food.

Hunting big animals is hard and dangerous work.

GRAY WOLF
Canis lupus

It Takes a Pack

Every spring, the alpha female finds or digs a safe den for her new pups. It might be underground, or in a hillside, or under a rock or the roots of a tree. While she's nursing the pups, the rest of us bring her food so she doesn't get hungry. When the pups get big enough to start playing outside, the whole pack helps take care of them, bringing them food to eat and sticks to play with, and teaching them how to be wolves. Everyone loves the pups!

Why Do Wolves Howl?

Wolves don't really howl at the moon. We just like to run around at night, and we howl with our heads back to help the sound carry. So why do we howl?

* To remind intruders to stay away. You can hear a howl through the forest up to six miles away, and even farther across open land!

* To find packmates who may have wandered off.

* For fun! I like howling with my family when we're excited about something — it's like a big, furry group hug.

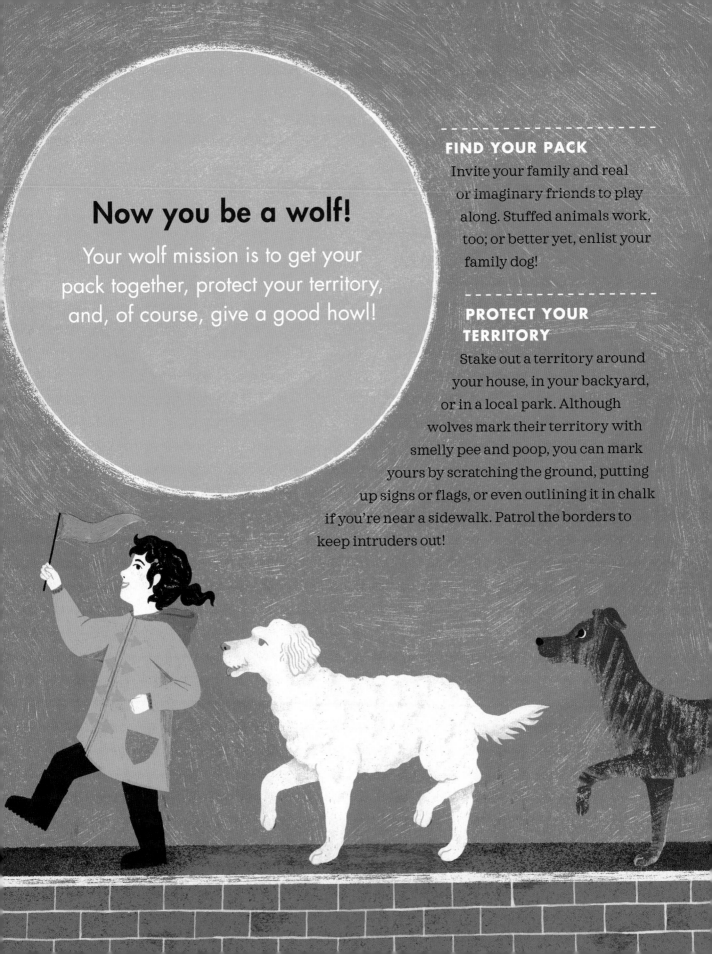

Now you be a wolf!

Your wolf mission is to get your pack together, protect your territory, and, of course, give a good howl!

FIND YOUR PACK

Invite your family and real or imaginary friends to play along. Stuffed animals work, too; or better yet, enlist your family dog!

PROTECT YOUR TERRITORY

Stake out a territory around your house, in your backyard, or in a local park. Although wolves mark their territory with smelly pee and poop, you can mark yours by scratching the ground, putting up signs or flags, or even outlining it in chalk if you're near a sidewalk. Patrol the borders to keep intruders out!

FOLLOW THE ALPHA

Pick one or two wolves in your pack to be the alphas. Everyone else must follow the alpha and do what he or she does. If the alpha sits, jumps, rolls over, or howls, the other wolves do, too.

TALK LIKE A WOLF

Imagine you look just like a wolf, with a tail and pointy ears. Try "talking" to your packmates by getting down on all fours and using wolf body language.

I'm the boss:

Hold your head and tail up high. Look confident and relaxed, and make eye contact with everyone in your pack. Growl and show your teeth if someone isn't listening.

I don't want to fight:

Keep your ears back, your tail tucked between your legs, and look away. You can also crouch to the ground so you look smaller, or roll over and show your belly.

Let's play!:

Keep your ears up and facing forward and your tail up and wagging, and make excited "play bows" by lowering your front half and keeping your bottom up in the air.

GROUP HOWL!

End a round of playing wolf with a group rally to remind everyone that you're all part of one big family. Get all the wolves in your pack to howl together, then wrestle around in a big, friendly pile. Bonus points if you can get your dog to howl along!

Ayhooooo!

ALL IN THE FAMILY

Gray wolves are the largest living member of the Canidae family. They're related to coyotes, dingoes, jackals, African wild dogs, and foxes. All pet dogs — from Great Danes to Chihuahuas — were domesticated from wild wolves!

SLIDE like a
PENGUIN

Hi there! I'm an emperor penguin. At almost four feet tall and up to 90 pounds, I'm by far the biggest penguin in the world. In fact, you and I could stand face to face and look each other in the eye.

We penguins are birds, but none of us can fly. Our wings are more like flippers, and we use them to race through the ocean chasing after fish. We're super-good swimmers.

EMPEROR PENGUIN
Aptenodytes forsteri

I live in ice-covered Antarctica, and let me tell you, that water is really, really cold. Fortunately, I have a couple of special adaptations that keep me from freezing to death. For example, if I look a little chubby, that's because I've got a nice thick layer of fat that helps keep my body heat from escaping. I also have stiff, dense, overlapping contour feathers covering my smaller, fluffy down feathers, and together they keep me extra warm and waterproof.

I can hold my breath for over 20 minutes!

PAPA TIME

When a mama penguin lays her single egg, she doesn't make a nest and sit on it like most birds. Nope, instead she passes the egg along to its father, and then she leaves to go hunting. Dad balances that egg on the tops of his feet for two whole months!

Now you be a penguin!

Your penguin mission is to keep you and your family cozy and warm in the icy weather! To feel more like a penguin, it helps to dress up in all black-and-white clothes.

EGG BALANCING

Find a medium-sized ball or a small stuffed animal. If you're outside, try a water balloon or snowball, depending on the season. This is your egg. Now balance it on the tops of your feet and try to slowly shuffle around and rock back on your heels like a papa penguin without letting your egg roll away!

Emperor penguin dads spend the winter standing on the windy open ice, huddling together with thousands of friends to keep themselves and their eggs warm. They don't eat or sit down the entire time!

"peep!"

FAIR-WEATHER BIRDS

Some kinds of penguins inhabit the warm southern coasts of Africa, Australia, and South America, as well as the Galapagos Islands. These warm-climate penguins don't need to worry so much about staying warm, but they still live next to the ocean where they hunt for fish.

BELLY SLIDE!

When they get sick of walking, penguins slide across the snow and ice on their bellies. You can, too! If it's winter and there is snow outside, get bundled up and build a snow hill to sled down face-first. If it's summer, set up a backyard water slide.

See how fast you can cruise on your belly!

wheee!

AFRICAN ELEPHANT
Loxodonta africana

KEEP COOL like an
ELEPHANT

Good day to you! I'm an African elephant. Can you tell that I'm the biggest, heaviest land animal in the world? I mean, just look at me! I'm bigger than your family car!

I couldn't say for sure, but I think we elephants probably have the coolest noses of any animal. My flexible, boneless trunk is made of pure muscle and is about five feet long. I use it to smell things, of course, but I can also use it to help me drink water or as a long hand when I'm looking for food.

Can you lift heavy objects, pluck a blade of grass, or give a friend a hug with your nose? I can!

I use my trunk to keep cool on hot days by spraying water, then dust, over my body to make a nice cool coat of mud to protect me from the sun. I can also use my amazing ears like giant fans to help me manage the heat — they're about four feet across!

I spray water on my back to cool off.

Herd Life

Our herds are led by an old matriarch, or boss mama. It's great being part of a herd — we're very loving, protective, and cooperative with each other. We work together to make group decisions, celebrate happy times, and grieve losses as a family.

What do you like to do with your family?

Our classic ivory **tusks** are actually specialized teeth, and we use them to dig up roots, rip off tree bark, and scare enemies.

An Elephant Never Forgets

It's true! We elephants have incredible memories. We can recognize other elephants we haven't seen in years and keep track of where everyone in our herd is at any given time. Our memories help us survive. For example, during droughts, when our usual watering holes dry up, our matriarchs remember how to get to other sources of water in faraway places.

Now you be an elephant!

Your elephant mission is to use your nose and ears to keep cool and your powerful memory to keep track of all your herd members. Put on your thinking cap!

HOSE NOSE!

Elephants use their trunks to suck up nearly two gallons of water at a time. They'll hold the water, then spray it out of their trunks and into their mouths when they want a drink. Sometimes they spray water on their backs to cool off or shoot it around just for fun. You can, too, with a regular old garden hose: head outside on a hot day, turn on the spigot, and wield that hose like it's your trunk!

MAKE AN ELEPHANT-EAR FAN

Cool yourself off on a hot day! Here's what you'll need:

* Card stock or poster board
* Paper and pencil
* Scissors
* Tape
* 2 craft sticks or rulers

Step 1

Using a pencil, outline an elephant ear on a piece of card stock. The ear should be at least as big as your head! Cut it out with scissors.

Step 2

Make a matching ear by tracing the first one onto another sheet of card stock. Cut out your second ear as well.

Step 3

Tape or glue each of your ears to its own sturdy wooden craft stick or ruler.

Now fan yourself with your ears and see how much they cool you off!

WHO'S THAT HANDSOME FACE?
Did you know elephants are one of only a few animals who can recognize their own reflections in a mirror?!

TEST YOUR MEMORY

A matriarch elephant can keep track of up to 30 of her companions at any given time, even when they're spread out foraging or hanging around a watering hole. How good is your memory?

Use the elephant shape below as a guide to trace or draw ten little elephants and cut them out. Make your elephants unique by coloring each one a different color or giving it a special name.

Place each elephant in a different spot around the room. Now take a break and go do something else for a few minutes. When you come back into the room, see if you can remember where everyone in your herd is. For an extra challenge, use more elephants, or watch someone else place them around the room and see if you can still remember where to find them!

TRACE
THIS
SHAPE!

LITTLE BROWN BAT
Myotis lucifugus

SEE like a
BAT

Greetings, reader! I'm a little brown bat. No really, that's my actual name! You may have heard that we bats are blind, but that isn't true.

We have eyes, and they mostly work just fine. But, since we're nocturnal animals and move around only at night, we come with another, extra-special way to "see" in the dark. It's called echolocation (say "ek-o-lo-KAY-shun"), and it's awesome...

You've heard an echo, right? Like when you yell into a big empty room or across a lake and hear your own voice come back at you? Well, that's basically how I get around in the dark without bumping into things. As I zoom through the air, I send little beepy-squeak noises into the air in front of me.

Sounds travel like waves in water, so when one of my beeps hits a tree, cave wall, or fluttering moth, the sound bounces back to me as an echo. I use these echoes to figure out how big an object is, how far away it is, and if it's moving. I can even tell if the object is soft, hard, or squishy, just by listening for that echo.

I actually *see* with sound!

Now you be a bat!

Your bat mission is to use your superpower of echolocation to find your way around and track down a delicious meal.

MOSQUITO HUNT

Many kinds of bats eat insects — lots of insects! In fact, a bat can gobble up thousands of mosquitoes every night, saving humans from countless itchy bites! Get ready to go on a mosquito hunt ...

Round up some friends and clear a room of furniture, or head outside. Pick one person to be the bat, one to be the mosquito. Everyone else can be trees or rocks or whatever objects they want to be. The goal is to see if the bat can find the mosquito using sound alone.

Blindfold the bat. Now have the mosquito and all the objects spread out and quietly stand in one place as the bat slowly walks around making squeaky sounds.

If you're an object and the bat stands facing you, clap to echo back at them so they know you're there. If you're the mosquito and the bat squeaks while it's facing you, make a loud buzzing sound. The bat should avoid running into objects while it walks toward the buzzing mosquito.

What made it easier or harder for the bat to catch its dinner?

Note: You can still play this game if you have only one partner. Just forget about the objects and have one person be the bat and the other be the mosquito.

BZZZzz!

HANGING OUT
We bats rest upside down, hanging by our feet, usually from cave ceilings, from tree branches, or from under bridges and house eaves. Feel what it's like to nap like a bat by dangling upside down from your knees on monkey bars at the playground.

How does the world look from a bat's-eye view?

23

SQUEEZE like an OCTOPUS

8 ARMS, 3 HEARTS
Everyone knows octopuses have eight arms, but did you also know that we have **three hearts**? One heart actually stops beating while we swim. That's why we usually prefer to walk, crawl, or drift, unless we need to move really fast.

Hello, and nice to meet you! I'm an octopus, and I just happen to be the biggest of my kind: a giant Pacific octopus. Like all octopuses, I'm an invertebrate, meaning I have no bones at all.

My ocean-dwelling cousins and I may look like bags of mush, but we're actually really strong and really smart.

And guess what? We don't just think with our brains — we also think with our arms.

See, my eight arms kind of have a mind of their own. They can search for food and figure out how to open clams while the rest of me is focused on something else. It would be like if one of your hands could play the piano while the other drew a picture, all while you were solving a math problem in your head.

We can also use our arms like legs to push off the ocean floor and sort of "walk" around. And they're so strong, we can pull and lift things many, many times heavier than our own weight.

GIANT PACIFIC OCTOPUS
Enteroctopus dofleini

3...2...1...Blast Off!

I don't have a tail or big fins to help me swim, but when I do need to get somewhere fast, I have a super-cool trick to use. Have you ever seen a rocket launched into space? Well, that's kind of how I move! It's called jet propulsion.

wHOOSH!

Imagine what happens when you blow up a balloon and let it go: the force of the air coming out makes the balloon fly all around the room, right? I'm like that balloon, only I fill up part of my body with water instead of air and then squeeze it out of a small hole, or siphon.

Off I go!

And if a shark or other predator gets too close, I've got another great getaway trick. I can shoot out a stream of blackish ink to create a dark cloud in the water that confuses my attacker as I make my escape.

SUCKERS!
Each of my arms has over 200 round suction cups. I use them to feel, taste, and identify the world around me, as well as to grip on to prey, rocks, and other objects.

Now you be an octopus!

Your octopus mission is to use your super-smart brain and super-flexible body to get out of any tricky situation. Start feeling like an octopus by stretching your body, waving your arms around, and curling your fingers up one at a time.

GET READY TO SQUEEZE

Octopuses are skilled at wriggling their boneless bodies into all sorts of tight spaces. Pretend you don't have any hard bones, and see how flexible you can be! Try folding yourself into an empty box or cupboard, or make a snug den out of blankets.

Squeeze between the legs of a chair or through a crack in a door that is barely open. Wriggle your way through any other tight spaces you can find, but just be careful you don't get stuck!

INK EXPERIMENT

Watch how octopuses use ink to hide from and confuse predators! For this experiment, you'll need these things:

* A clear glass jar or vase
* A small object like a rock or marble — or even a tiny toy octopus!
* Blue, purple, or black liquid food coloring (or watered-down washable tempera paint and an eyedropper)

Step 1
Fill up a clear glass vase or jar with clean water.

Step 2
Place your small object or tiny toy octopus in the glass and allow it to sink to the bottom. Notice how easy it is to see your object through the clear water.

Step 3
Now add a few drops of food coloring "ink" to the container and watch how the water changes color. Keep adding ink until you can't see your object. How much ink did it take?

Step 4
Refill your jar with clean water and quickly add one big squirt of ink to see how a startled octopus can create a cloud of instant darkness and escape!

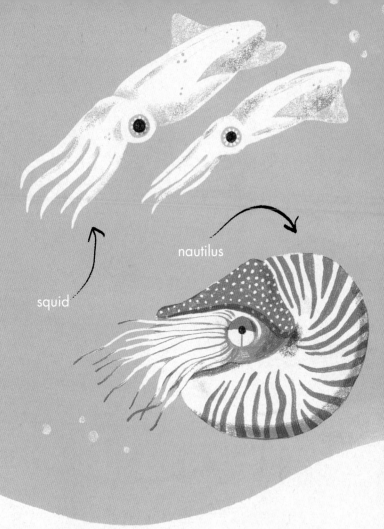

CEPHALOPODS

Octopuses are a type of cephalopod (say "SEF-a-lo-pod"), a class of ocean-dwelling animals that also includes squids, cuttlefish, and nautiluses. These animals all have big heads, boneless bodies, and multiple sets of arms or tentacles. The biggest known cephalopod is the colossal squid, a rarely seen deepwater creature that can grow over 40 feet long — that's bigger than a school bus!

squid

nautilus

ESCAPE ARTISTS

In aquariums, octopuses have been known to solve puzzles, use tools, navigate mazes, unscrew jars, and open childproof containers. Now and then we even escape our tanks!

What kinds of puzzles are you good at?

RATTLE like a
RATTLESNAKE

NEED A NEW SKIN?

Your human skin grows as you grow, so it always fits just right. But snake skin can't really stretch like that, so it gets too tight as we grow bigger. Luckily, I can just rub my head on something rough until the old layer of skin snags and tears. Then I slither forward and let the skin peel off behind me. Every time I shed I get a new segment on my rattle!

Greetingsssss . . . oh, please, don't run away! I promise to warn you if you're getting too close. See, I'm a rattlesnake.

That's what the rattles on our tails are for — to tell you to step back so you don't get hurt! We don't want to bite anyone we aren't planning on eating (and we're definitely not eating you), so the rattle is just a way to ask you to give us some space.

To be honest, my bite really does hurt. I'm a venomous snake, which means my hollow fangs contain a kind of toxin made to kill my prey, such as a rat or a ground squirrel, very quickly. When I'm slithering around looking for something to eat, I flick my forked tongue in and out of my mouth to taste the smell of prey in the air. When it's time to eat, I don't even chew my food, I just swallow it whole — *gulp*.

My mouth can open so wide, I can eat animals bigger than my head!

DIAMONDBACK RATTLESNAKE
Crotalus atrox

Now you be a rattlesnake!

Your rattlesnake mission is to get around by slithering and to use your scary rattle to warn others to stay away.

MAKE A RATTLE

How do you let people know you need some space? If you're a rattlesnake, you use your rattle. You can make a simple rattle out of just about any small container. Try a plastic egg, an old pill bottle, or another small, hard container. Fill your container about halfway with dried rice or beans or anything small and hard. Shake your rattle to tell others to stay away when you want to be left alone!

You can drop your rattle into the toe of a sock, wrap a string or a rubber band around the other end to close it up, and have someone help you attach it to your pants with a safety pin.

How far can you slither across the floor by wiggling from side to side?

REPTILE WORLD

All snakes are reptiles. We're cold-blooded animals, which means we can't keep ourselves warm or cool without help from the sun or shade. That's why you'll often find us basking in the morning sun or hiding under a rock on a hot day.

There are over 10,000 different types of reptiles on Earth, including crocodiles, alligators, turtles, and lizards. They come in all shapes and sizes, and some even look like dragons!

Don't forget to flick your tongue to taste the air . . .

BUILD like a
BOWERBIRD

A **bower** isn't really a **nest**. Nests provide birds with cozy places to rest, lay their eggs, and raise their chicks. But a bower is more like an exciting stage where I can show off my extra-special skills.

What extra-special skills do you have?

Hi there! I'm a bowerbird. I live in the tropical forests and shrublands of Australia and Papua New Guinea.

I don't mean to brag, but I am a pretty amazing artist. I build tall structures called bowers on the forest floor using sticks, woven grasses, and moss. Only male bowerbirds build nests.

I have a unique sense of style.

Once I finish building my fancy bower, I go looking for bright objects to use as decorations. I like to gather flowers, berries, pebbles, or shells — hundreds of them! — to display on the ground in front of my bower.

The decorations might be all different colors or I might pick one color — like blue — and gather anything I can find in that one shade. And just as you probably like your bedroom to look a certain way, I spend many hours arranging my treasures to make sure everything is perfect.

GREAT BOWERBIRD
Chlamydera nuchalis

Creative Builders

There are many different kinds of bowerbirds, and each type has its own style. Some bowers look like tunnels, while others look like tents or two walls standing next to each other.

Which bower style do you like best?

AVENUE

MAYPOLE

THATCHED

DOUBLE-MAYPOLE

Here are some things that have been found in real bowers.

beetles

snail shells

berries

pinecones

seeds

drinking straws

flowers

* gum wrappers
* bottle caps
* bits of string
* stones
* milk bottle caps
* feathers
* clothespins
* broken glass

* ballpoint pens
* spoons
* coins
* paper clips
* shiny jewelry
* pieces of plastic

What would you use to decorate your bower?

Now you be a bowerbird!

Your bowerbird mission is to be super-creative and build the best bower you can to show off your skills.

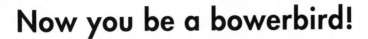

BUILD YOUR BOWER

You can make a bower out of almost anything.

Outdoors...

Try sticking two branches or broomsticks in the ground, about an arm's width apart.

Lean or weave smaller sticks and grasses against those branches, to make the walls bigger and form a kind of tunnel. You might need to use a little string to hold it all together.

You could also use fence posts or tree trunks as your bower's tall walls.

Now go for a walk and collect colorful objects that catch your eye. Display these objects on the ground in front of your bower.

In your house...

Drape a blanket over two chairs or across a doorframe to make an archway. Or use a large cardboard box with its ends cut off.

You can find lots of good decorations inside, too. Large colorful beads, blocks, small toys, Legos, ribbons, and crayons are good additions. You can also cut up pieces of brightly colored paper into different shapes. Then arrange them by color or shape into little piles in front of your stage.

Bowerbirds aren't the only animals that collect stuff. Decorator crabs pluck things from the ocean floor and stick them onto their backs to disguise themselves from predators.

When you play dress-up, what do you like to wear?

Now the exciting part!

PUT ON A SHOW

As a male bowerbird, I have to wait for a curious female to come around and look at my colorful collection. Then I can use my bower as a stage where I put on a show. I'll strut around, bouncing up and down and bobbing my head. I'll shake my tail feathers as I do a little dance, and sing my song to try to impress her.

How will you show off YOUR hard work?

Give visitors a tour of your bower. Maybe offer them a little snack of fruit. Then it's time to perform...

Jump!

dance!

STRUT!

ENGINEER like a
BEAVER

My family and I build a cozy **lodge** to live in on a riverbank, a lakeshore, or an island. Our lodge may look like a big, messy pile of sticks, grass, and mud from the outside, but it's home to us. It even has a secret underwater entrance!

Hi! It's true, I look a little wobbly when I waddle over land, but in the water where I live, I'm as graceful as a fish.

But I'm no fish — I'm a beaver! My big, paddle-shaped tail and webbed hind feet act like a rudder and fins to help me swim, and my soft, glossy brown fur is waterproof, so I never get chilly, even in cold water.

If I can't find the perfect spot for a house alongside a lake, pond, or river, I may use my excellent engineering skills to build a home in the water and create a habitat. Of course, I can't use human tools like shovels and saws, but that's okay. I don't need them.

I have the perfect tools — my teeth.

My teeth are so strong and my jaws are so powerful, I can gnaw right through wood and even cut down whole trees! Then I haul the logs and branches over to a stream, weave them together, and plaster them with mud to build a dam that stops the flow of water. The water starts to back up and overflow, flooding the surrounding forest, field, or meadow, and eventually creating a nice big pond for me to live in.

secret entrance

NORTH AMERICAN BEAVER
Castor canadensis

Now you be a beaver!

Your beaver mission is to use your amazing engineering skills to build the perfect dam and make a new pond habitat for you and your family.

MAKE YOUR OWN RIVER

If you're at the beach, you can carve your own river in the wet sand. Or if you're in your backyard, you can make a mini-waterway by digging a trench and turning on the hose a little bit at one end. Then just build your dam like you would in a real stream.

BUILD A DAM

If you're outside, see if you can find a little brook or stream. Pick a spot to build your dam, and then gather rocks and sticks to use as building materials. Start on one edge of the stream and work your way across, laying down a sturdy layer of larger rocks and sticks. Leave a little channel open at the end so the water can keep moving downstream for now.

Add more layers to your dam as needed. When your dam is higher than the flowing water, it's time to block that last little side channel. Did your dam hold? Is the water rising and creating a little pool? Fill in any leaks with small rocks, mud, or moss.

CHOMP LIKE A BEAVER

If all that work made you hungry, use your front teeth to gnaw through some carrot sticks, radishes, or pretzel rods, pretending they're tree trunks!

Beaver teeth never stop growing! Luckily, all that gnawing wears their teeth down as they grow, so they never get too long.

Chomp, chomp, chomp...

SNEAK like a
LEOPARD

Oh, hey. Were you just checking out my spots? I don't mind. I'm a leopard, and spots are kind of my thing. RAWR!

My dark markings are actually called rosettes, because they look a little like a blossoming rose. But I don't wear them just because they look good. You might think those spots would make me stand out like a sore thumb, but actually, they imitate how the sun shines through leaves to create dappled shadows. Believe it or not, my markings work as camouflage to help me hide from enemies and quietly hunt my prey.

But my spots aren't the only reason I'm a good hunter.

I'm also really strong, very patient, and super-stealthy.

Have you ever watched a house cat stalk a mouse or a toy by lying low to the ground and slowly sneaking up on it? Then you have a pretty good idea of my hunting style — except I usually go after bigger prey like antelope and deer.

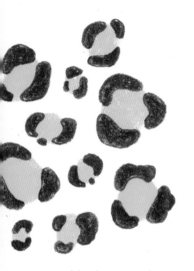

Just like how each human has a unique set of fingerprints, every leopard has its own special rosette pattern!

LEOPARD
Panthera pardus

Expert Tree Climbers

I'm great at climbing trees! Sometimes I'll jump out of one to pounce on my unsuspecting prey. And then just to make sure a hyena or lion doesn't steal my lunch, I'll drag the whole thing up into my tree, so I can eat it in peace, or maybe save it for later. This type of food hiding is called caching (say "cash-ing").

A mama leopard might hide her cubs in a hollow tree, cozy rock den, or small cave to keep them safe.

Where do you feel most safe?

caching food

BIG CATS

Leopards are the smallest of the "true" big cats, followed by jaguars, lions, and finally tigers, who are the largest cats in the world. Cougars, snow leopards, clouded leopards, and cheetahs are also large-sized cats, but unlike true big cats, they cannot roar.

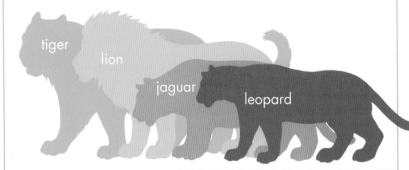

tiger

lion

jaguar

leopard

Now you be a leopard!

Your leopard mission is to be super-sneaky and to use your expert climbing skills to find a special spot to eat your lunch and keep watch.

CAMOUFLAGE YOURSELF

Ever wish you could make yourself invisible? Try some camouflage! For starters, get some yellow, orange, and black face paint and ask an adult to give you a classic spotted leopard face. Put on matching clothing, too, if you have it. But also keep in mind that the key to camouflage is blending in. A leopard's spots help it stay hidden under shadowy leaves and grasses, but if you're playing leopard on a snowy day or on a sandy beach, you can wear whatever clothing best helps you hide.

HIDE AND STALK

Leopards use slyness and patience to sneak up on their prey. You can stalk your "prey," too. First find someone or something to sneak up on — like a distracted parent, a sleeping pet, or even a stuffed animal. Crouch down close to the floor, and slowly, quietly, on all fours, creep up on your prey, inch by inch. When you're nearly close enough to touch them, leap out to surprise them! (But never grab a sleeping pet — animals don't like to be startled.)

READY, SET...

THE ART OF HIDING

Lots of animals use camouflage to hide.
There are moths that look like tree bark,
insects that look like flowers, frogs that look
like leaves, and fish that look like coral.
And get this — some octopuses, squid, and
cuttlefish can even change their skin color
to blend in with the scenery wherever they
go. It's almost like being invisible!

CLIMB AND CACHE

Leopards love to climb trees, and they're really good
at it! Find a nearby tree with low-hanging branches.
Monkey bars and jungle gyms work, too, and even a
couch or bunk bed will do in a pinch. Carefully pull
yourself up onto a comfortable perch and survey
your surroundings.

Take a pretend nap if you're feeling tired. You can
even take a snack up to your perch and eat it there!

caching
food

SING like a
HUMPBACK
WHALE

WHAT'S FOR DINNER?

Instead of teeth, our mouths are full of baleen, which is kind of like a big, bristly comb. When we eat, we scoop up a bunch of water into our mouths, then strain it back out through our baleen. This traps the teeny-tiny animals we eat (plankton and krill) inside our mouths.

Woo wooop brrooop! I'm a humpback whale. Though I may look like a really, really big fish, I'm actually a mammal, just like you.

That means I can't breathe underwater, and I have to come up to the surface to suck air in through my blowhole, the same way you breathe through your nose.

I have baleen instead of teeth.

Every humpback whale has its own unique set of markings on the underside of its tail, or **fluke**. These markings are like fingerprints. Whale biologists take photographs of them so they can tell different whales apart.

We tend to live alone, but sometimes we travel and feed together in groups called pods.

We humpbacks are really famous for our long, beautiful, complex songs. That's right, we sing!

While both males and females communicate with different noises, or vocalizations, only males truly sing. Sometimes we sing alone, and sometimes we sing together, moaning, wailing, clicking, and groaning with our blowholes. All the males in one area sing the same song, which can be heard from far away through the water. It's kind of a secret why we sing, so I can't tell you for sure why, but scientists think it might be a way to attract mates, challenge other males, or simply explore the sea around us and find out what other whales are close by.

Why do **you** think we sing?

HUMPBACK WHALE
Megaptera novaengliae

Now you be a whale!

Your whale mission is to make up a beautiful whale song that's all about you.

- -

GET TALKING AND SINGING

Instead of using words, see if you can communicate simple phrases like "come here" and "hello" using beeps, grunts, and thwop sounds. Then make up your own whale song! It can be just a series of sounds, or you can make up words to go with them. Try singing about who you are, where you're from, and what it's like to live in your little corner of the great big ocean. Hum your song underwater and see if your friends can hear it!

When you are at a pool, a lake, or even just in your bathtub, you can practice your whale song while you swim.

brrooop!

SPLASH AROUND

Humpback whales are amazing swimmers. Try breaching like a whale by leaping out of the water and crashing back down on your side. Stretch out your arms like fins and spin around in a spiral. Lean back and slap your feet against the water's surface like a whale tail coming down.

If you can't be in the water, don't worry, just lay a comfy blanket on the floor (a blue one if you can!) and imagine you are in the ocean.

dive!

Thrash!

roll!

WESTERN HONEYBEE
Apis mellifera

DANCE like a
HONEYBEE

Bzzzz! May I ask you a question? Did you eat any fruits or vegetables today? If so, did you know that I probably helped that food grow? Please allow me to explain. I'm a honeybee.

In the spring and summer, I get all the food I need from flowers.

I crawl right in and slurp up their sweet, juicy nectar with my special tongue, and while I'm there I also collect sticky yellow pollen.

But something else happens as I buzz from flower to flower. Some of that dusty pollen I picked up in one rubs off inside another. That's called pollination, and it's really important. If a plant isn't pollinated, it can't produce fruit or seeds, and without seeds, there would be no baby plants. So you see, by pollinating flowers, I help plants grow.

I pick pollen up on my legs.

YUMMY FOODS THAT NEED THE BEES

* Apples
* Avocados
* Almonds
* Cherries
* Cucumbers
* Blueberries
* Oranges
* Onions
* Pumpkins

I live in a big hive with thousands of my family members.

We have one **queen** who rules the hive and lays all the eggs.

QUEEN

HONEY TO SHARE
We turn raw nectar into delicious honey and store it in honeycomb chambers so we can eat it all winter long while we stay warm and cozy inside our hive.

DRONE

We also have a few brothers, called **drones.**

WORKER

My sisters and I do almost everything. **Workers** are all about teamwork.

Dancing for Dinner

When we find a patch of juicy flowers, we go home and tell our sisters where to find it. How do we tell them? By doing the **waggle dance** of course!

With this special dance, we can tell each other how far to go in what direction to find the flowers. If the patch has lots and lots of nectar, the dancer shows excitement by waggling really fast!

Now you be a bee!

Your honeybee mission is to pollinate flowers and show your friends where to find the sweetest nectar.

DO THE WAGGLE DANCE

Have a friend close her eyes for a minute. Look around for a flower in your yard, or hide a little snack if you are inside. Now pretend you're a bee, and you've got to tell the other bees in your hive where to find the nectar.

Do a waggle dance for your friend, pointing in the direction of the food. Dance longer if it is far away, and shake your bum faster if it's a really good treat! Did your fellow bee find the food?

HELP POLLINATE FLOWERS

As a bee, you also have the big job of pollinating plants to help them grow. Ready to give it a try? Grab a Q-tip, pipe cleaner, or cotton ball and head outside. Find a blooming plant, and look inside a flower to find the dusty yellow or orange pollen sitting on the anthers. Very gently, reach in and dab the pollen with your Q-tip. (You can use your fingers, too.) Then find another flower of the same kind and lightly rub the pollen you've captured onto the new flower's stigma, the long, skinny part in the center of the flower.

Congratulations, you've just helped that plant make a seed!

stigma

anther

THE BIRDS AND THE BEES
Did you know that hummingbirds pollinate flowers? And they do it while beating their wings 50 times per second!

SWEET FACTS ABOUT HONEY

* **Honey never goes bad!**
  In a sealed container, honey will stay good for thousands of years.

* **Honey helps heal!**
  Germs can't really grow in honey, so some people spread it on their cuts and burns, kind of like a liquid bandage.

* **Making honey is hard work!**
  Honeybees must visit nearly two million (2,000,000) flowers to get enough nectar to make just one pound of honey. No wonder we call them busy bees!

DRINK LIKE A BEE

Before your next snack, cut a simple flower shape out of a colorful piece of paper and slip it over a straw. Pretend the straw is your long bee tongue, and suck up your juice through the straw just like a bee sipping nectar!

COMMON RAVEN
Corvus corax

JOKE like a
RAVEN

Kraw! Kraw! Hey there, friend! I know I look like a backyard crow, but I'm actually a raven. You can think of me as crow's bigger cousin.

I love to play games!

We ravens are playful tricksters, and we love a good joke. You might see me teasing other animals, like pulling on a wolf's or dog's tail while they aren't looking! I might even steal the socks off your laundry line or try to unzip a backpack to look for treats if I'm feeling mischievous. And I love playing games, like sliding down snowbanks in winter.

We ravens are some of the smartest birds — and smartest animals — in the whole world.

I even know how to steal a fisherman's catch by pulling up the fishing line from the water! And we're one of just a few wild animals who know how to make and use tools, including our own toys. Sticks and pinecones are some of my favorites. I also love to play while I fly. I can dive, barrel roll, fly upside down, and do somersaults in midair!

RAVEN TALK
While I don't exactly sing, I can make 30 different kinds of sounds! I croak and kraw like a crow, but deeper. You may also hear me making gurgling croaks, shrill alarm calls, or loud knocking sounds. Tame ravens can even learn to say human words!

Can you croak and kraw like a raven?

Now you be a raven!

Your raven mission is to be a clever trickster. Get ready to have some sneaky fun!

- -

PLAY SOME TRICKS!

Sly ravens love to play tricks. Try sneaking up on a friend who isn't looking, and gently pull on their shirt before jumping away. Or play a trickster game with a sheet of stickers by seeing how many you can silently stick onto your parent, sibling, or friend without them noticing! And even though ravens can't exactly tell jokes, you know they would if they could.

What's your favorite joke?

ANIMALS AND TOOLS

Ravens and crows aren't the only animals who use tools. For example, sea otters use rocks to crack open hard shells. Gorillas sometimes use walking sticks to cross deep water, while chimpanzees and orangutans use sticks and leaves to collect honey from beehives and pull out ants and termites from their nests.

CATCH AND BALANCE

Ravens sometimes make their own toys by breaking twigs off branches to play catch with. Find your own small stick, pinecone, or other toy. Throw it in the air and catch it on the way down, or toss it to a friend. Now throw it a little higher and try jumping or spinning around before you catch it again. Can you balance your toy on your forearm, palm, shoulder, knee, or head?

STRIPED SKUNK
Mephitis mephitis

SPRAY like a
SKUNK

No, wait! Don't worry! Yes, I'm a skunk, but I promise I won't spray you. We skunks are gentle and shy, and we really don't want any trouble. But there's a reason people tend to keep their distance.

If you scare us or make us mad, we're not afraid to unleash the stink.

And what a stink it is! The scent glands under my tail hold my secret weapon — a super-smelly, yellowish liquid that I can spray like a squirt gun to hit a target over 10 feet away! This powerful spray can even make my enemies feel sick, or cause temporary blindness.

But the truth is, the average skunk would rather not have to spray you at all. See, after we get a handful of good sprays in, we're empty. Then we're pretty defenseless, because it can take days to make more spray and "reload." So spraying is our last resort. Before we spray we'll run through a little warning dance — hissing, stomping, jumping around, slapping our tails, and even sometimes doing a little handstand, all to try and scare you off.

BLIND AS A . . . SKUNK?
Skunks can barely see more than 10 feet ahead, and that's one reason why we often get hit by cars. So if you're riding in a car at night, please keep an eye out for us! We can't see you, but you might see us!

Fair Warning

The pattern of our black-and-white fur also tells predators to stay away. It's called warning coloration, and it's kind of like the opposite of camouflage. It helps advertise to the world that we're dangerous. In fact, my classic white stripes run from my neck down to my tail like two big arrows pointing right to source of my stink!

So, I have my colors and my warning dance to tell others to stay away.

How do you let people know when **you** *want to be left alone?*

COLOR CODE
Other animals use colors as warning signs, too. Poison dart frogs are among the most poisonous animals in the world, and their bright colors act like a big blinking danger sign: if you eat me, you'll die!

Skunk Pile!

Most skunks are about the size of house cats, and we usually live alone (unless we're mothers raising our babies, called kits). Sometimes, though, during a cold winter, a group of 12 or so females might den together underground in a big, snuggly pile to keep warm. We don't really hibernate, but we do spend most of the winter denned up, taking long naps and not eating.

Now you be a skunk!

Your skunk mission is to let others know you want to be left alone.

CREATE A WARNING LOOK

A skunk's white stripes let predators know it has a dangerous defensive weapon ready to go. How would you dress or paint your face if you wanted to warn others to stay away? Dress in stripes like a skunk or in bright danger colors like yellow and red. Paint big eyebrows on your face, sharp fangs, or anything else that helps you look like a scary animal nobody should mess with.

DESIGN A DEFENSIVE DANCE

Design your own "keep away" dance routine that lets your family and friends know you want some space. Try shaking your bottom, flapping your arms, stomping your feet, spinning around, standing on your hands, or any other move you can think of! When someone comes near you, repeat your warning dance a couple of times to scare them off.

And if that doesn't work, get ready to spray . . .

Foxes and wolves have learned not to attack us, but a lot of dogs don't seem to get the message. If one of us does spray your nosy dog, give her a bath in hydrogen peroxide, baking soda, and dishwashing soap to help get rid of the stench.

SPRAYERS

Skunks aren't the only animals who spray to defend themselves. Spitting cobras shoot poisonous flying venom from their fangs, and bombardier beetles launch dangerous boiling hot chemicals from their bottoms! Horned lizards will even shoot blood out of their eyes!

MAKE YOUR OWN SPRAY

You can make your own sprayer by filling up a spray bottle or squirt gun with water. Add a drop or two of an essential oil like lavender, tea tree, lemon, or peppermint to your sprayer to get a bit of a scent that won't make too much of a stink. When someone ignores your defensive dance and gets too close, give them a little spray!

TRANSFORM like a
FROG

THIN SKIN
We frogs can breathe through our delicate skin. Our skin is much thinner than yours, and very **permeable**, which means it can absorb water, minerals, and even oxygen.

Welcome to my pond! Yep, I'm a frog. Frogs come in all sorts of shapes, sizes, and colors, and we live on every continent except Antarctica (brrrrr!). In fact, I bet you've got some of us living in your neighborhood.

As for me, I'm a Columbia spotted frog. See my spotted back? All frogs, as well as toads and salamanders, are amphibians. That means we live some of our life in the water, and some of it on land. We're also cold-blooded like fish and reptiles. That means we depend on outside temperatures to warm or cool us, which is why you'll often see us warming ourselves in a patch of sunlight. Do you think I'm funny looking?

These big bulgy eyes help me look all around without having to move my head.

I hunt for dinner using my soft, thick tongue coated with super-sticky saliva. When I see a tasty insect hop or buzz by, I shoot out my tongue and snatch it up before it knows what happened!

COLUMBIA SPOTTED FROG
Rana luteiventris

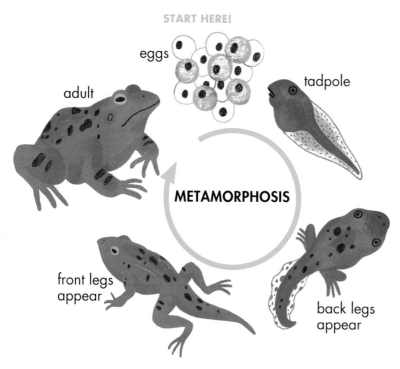

START HERE!

eggs

tadpole

adult

METAMORPHOSIS

front legs appear

back legs appear

The Life of a Frog

Like most frogs, I started my life as one of a bunch of eggs floating in freshwater. Before long, I hatched into a legless tadpole and raced around the water, breathing water through my gills. As I grew into the handsome, long-legged adult that I am, my lungs developed so I can breathe air. Now I mostly live on land.

This transformation from egg to tadpole to adult is called metamorphosis.

We Love to Sing!

Frogs make all kinds of noises. We use our loudest calls to scare enemies and to attract mates by saying "Hey! Over here!" You may think some of our calls sound strange, like a cartoon boing, a chirping bird, a finger running down the teeth of a comb, or even a car honking its horn, but they are music to our ears.

Now you be a frog!

Your frog mission is to use your legs to jump extra far, your long tongue to snatch up food, and your beautiful voice to call to other frogs. For extra frog fun, hang out near a pool or lake where you can go in and out of the water!

TRANSFORM YOURSELF

Go through the motions of frog metamorphosis!

1. Start off curled into a ball like a tiny egg.

3. Finally, you can "grow" your legs, and then your arms. *Now hop all around!*

2. After a few moments, slowly stretch out as if you've just hatched. Remember, young tadpoles don't have legs yet, so you'll have to wiggle around without using your arms or legs.

BIGGEST AND SMALLEST

The smallest known frog in the world is a little fellow from New Guinea who is only a third of an inch long — so tiny it can sit on a single dime with a few of its friends! Meanwhile, the goliath frog of Cameroon, Africa, is the biggest frog on Earth. It's over a foot long from snout to bottom and can weigh seven pounds!

LEAP, FROG!

Frogs are some of the best jumpers in the world. Most can leap over 20 times their length, and some tree frogs can jump over 150 times their length — that would be like you jumping a whole city block!

You'd better start practicing. Mark a starting point with chalk if you're on the sidewalk, a stick or ribbon if you're on the grass, or a piece of tape on the floor if you're inside. From a squatting position, see how far you can hop, and mark the spot where you land. Have a contest with your friends, or try to beat your own personal long jump record!

USE YOUR TONGUE

Set popcorn or pieces of small, dry cereal on a clean tabletop or plate. These are your "lunch flies." Bring your face close to your snack without touching it, then quickly flick your tongue out and see if you can catch one!

FROG CALLING

Go outside on a spring night near some freshwater and listen for frogs calling. If you have access to a recording device, take a recording and then play it back over the water. Sit down, keep still, and see if any frogs come close to investigate.

It's okay if you don't have a recorder or any frogs in your neighborhood — make up your own personal frog call using whatever sounds, words, or instruments you like!

GRAZE like a
DEER

Are you wondering about the **white-tailed** part of my name? Well, the underside of my tail is bright white. I lift it up and hold it high like a flag as I quickly bound away from danger!

Oh, hello. I'm sure you've seen me around the neighborhood, and I've certainly seen you. I'm your local white-tailed deer.

We deer are very adaptable and can make a home almost anywhere, including your backyard! But our favorite spots are places where fields and forests meet. The woods provide us with shelter, while open fields make for good grazing.

We deer take our eating very seriously!

Mostly, we're herbivores, which means we just eat plants. I love eating leaves, but I'll browse on just about any shrub, twig, nut, fruit, lichen, grass, or farm crop I come across. I've got flat teeth made for grinding up food.

By now you've probably noticed these big pointy things growing out of my head, right? It's okay to stare. I'm proud of them! They're called antlers, and only male deer, called bucks, grow them. I grow a new pair every single year!

WHITE-TAILED DEER
Odocoileus virginianus

Now you be a deer!

Your deer mission is to forage everywhere to find delicious food.

- -

GO FORAGING

Deer spend a lot of time foraging for plants to eat, so get ready to set out on your own foraging mission. Plant food is all around you!

In the garden

If it's summer and you have an organic garden, crouch down and nibble on lettuce leaves or snap peas.

What is your favorite vegetable to graze on?

For a quick pair of antlers, find a couple of branching twigs and hold them up to your head. You can even try scratching the ground with them or rubbing them against tree trunks like bucks do in the fall!

At the farmers' market or grocery store

Help an adult pick out veggies you think a deer would like to eat. Back at home, try eating your carrot sticks, salad, or corn on the cob without using your hands! And don't forget to grind your teeth!

In the wild

Find a knowledgeable adult to help you identify, forage for, and prepare wild plants to eat. Look for dandelion greens, violets, or nettles in spring, wild blueberries and blackberries in the summer, and apples in the fall. Just remember, not all plants are safe for humans to eat, so always check with an adult before you munch!

Baby deer are called **fawns** and have white spots.

Female deer are called **does**.

HORNS ARE NOT ANTLERS!
Antlers and horns are two different things. Antlers are branch shaped and are grown by bucks and some other animals like moose, elk, and caribou. Horns, on the other hand, don't branch and, unlike antlers, never fall off — in fact, most keep growing as long as the animal lives. Goats, cows, and sheep have horns, not antlers.

Click, Print, Cut, Play!

Visit www.storey.com/animal-masks
Download these 13 *Howl like a Wolf!* masks and dress up like your favorite animal.

WOLF

PENGUIN

ELEPHANT

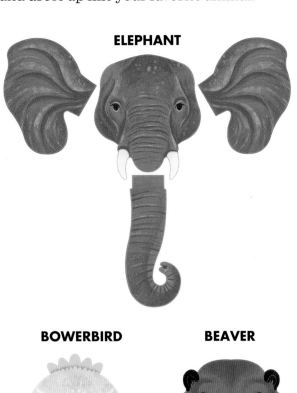

BAT

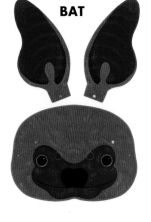

RATTLESNAKE

BOWERBIRD

BEAVER

LEOPARD

HONEYBEE

RAVEN

SKUNK

FROG

DEER